DRESSES AND DRESSMAKING
From the Late Georgians to the Edwardians

Pam Inder

AMBERLEY

First published 2018

Amberley Publishing
The Hill, Stroud
Gloucestershire, GL5 4EP

www.amberleybooks.com

British Library Cataloguing in Publication Data.
A catalogue record for this book is available from the British Library.

ISBN 978 1 4456 7242 7 (print)
ISBN 978 1 4456 7243 4 (ebook)

Typesetting and Origination by Amberley Publishing.
Printed in Great Britain.

Contents

Acknowledgements

My special thanks go to Sarah Nicol at the Leicestershire Museums Collections Resource Centre for her help, hard work and endless patience. I would also like to thank Fiona Graham, Simon Lake and Sarah Levitt at Leicester Arts and Museum Service and the staff at Leicestershire Record Office for all their help and support.

Sources of Illustrations

The following images are provided courtesy of:

Leicester City Council Arts and Museum Service – 7, 9–11a, 12, 34, 64a&b, 78d
Leicestershire County Council Museums Resource Centre – 1, 3–5a, 16–19, 24, 25, 29–33a, 37, 37a, 39, 39a&b, 40–42b, 44–45a, 48, 48a&b, 51, 54, 58, 60–62a, 67, 67a&b, 69–73a, 75, 77, 78, 84–93, 95–97,100, 104, 109, 109a&b, 111, 116
Leicestershire County Council Museums Environment and Heritage Service (Image Leicestershire) – 6, 13, 14, 15, 53, 114, 115, 117
Leicestershire and Rutland County Record Office – 8, 22, 23, 38, 46, 49, 52, 65, 66, 74
The Victoria and Albert Museum – 26–28, 35, 43, 57, 59, 68
Wikimedia – 110
Eric Kilby (Wikimedia) – 88a

Money

There are various references to prices in the text. These are all in 'old' money – pounds (£), shillings (s) and pence (d). There were 12 pence in a shilling and 20 shillings in a pound. It is impossible to convert prices into modern money with any degree of accuracy; however, throughout the period under review, £1 a week was considered a 'good' wage, one on which a respectable working man could support a wife and children, though many men, and most women, earned considerably less.

Measurements

Measurements are given in Imperial units – inches, feet and yards. 1 inch = just over 2½ centimetres. There were 12 inches in a foot = 30½ centimetres, and 3 feet in a yard = 91½ centimetres.

Introduction

Clothes are the stuff of everyday life. Looking at what people wore tells us about craftsmanship, social attitudes, ideals of beauty, family life, trade, technological developments, the changing role of women and more besides. Even people who know nothing about history can imagine wearing the garments they see in museum showcases and can get some idea of how uncomfortable and impractical many of them were.

Studying dress also brings some surprises. We find, for instance, that the much-talked-about '18-inch waist' existed mainly in fiction. True, the population as a whole got taller, heavier and healthier in the twentieth century as a result of improved diet and living conditions, but though many nineteenth-century dresses are small, virtually none have 18-inch waists. Surviving garments show us that women in the nineteenth century came in all shapes and sizes: there were small women, tall women, skinny women, and women who were frankly obese.

We also discover that not all women were talented seamstresses. Sewing formed part of a girl's education, but not all girls were good at it. Dresses survive that are beautifully cut and constructed, but there are a significant number of others that are clumsily made and crudely stitched. Similarly, some dresses have been exquisitely repaired, while in others tears have been inexpertly cobbled together.

Of course, not everyone had the chance to learn to sew. In 1843 the Children's Employment Commission published in their report a letter from Dr Shaw, a physician at Leicester Infirmary. He wrote:

1. A dress of brown striped wool, *c.* 1860. This is shown on a hanger because it was impossible to find a figure to fit it. The lady who wore it was about 5 feet 3 inches tall and had a 45-inch waist!

> In this town there is a considerable number of dress-makers employed by the poorer classes. This depends on the fact of the wives of the mechanics being in general entirely ignorant of all domestic knowledge, and who consequently are unable to make their own dresses, etc.

Such women had probably started work as children and had little, if any, schooling. It is clear, too, that our ancestors did not all have immaculate taste. Fashion writers urged their readers to choose quiet colours that would not date and ring the changes with lace and jewellery and bright ribbons, but many women ignored that advice. Dresses were usually made to the wearer's specifications and there is no shortage of over-decorated dresses made from garish fabrics, and obviously not everyone was able to envisage what would result from their chosen combination of fabric and trimmings. Clara Dare's dress is a case in point. Clara was born in 1848, the youngest daughter of Joseph Dare and his wife, Mary. Joseph was employed by the Unitarian congregation as a 'domestic missionary' to work among the poor of Leicester. Sometime in the late 1860s, when she was about twenty, Clara had a new winter dress made for her by a visiting dressmaker. It is a two-piece garment made of quite a coarse woollen cloth with a fine purple stripe, with an unflattering square neckline and is trimmed with heavy purple fringe and braid. The story goes that Clara hated the dress and immediately handed it over to her nieces for their dressing-up box!

" These Dresses are very well in their way, but they make us all appear the same size. Why, a Girl might be as thin as a Whipping-post, and yet be taken for a Decent Figure."

2. *Punch*, 31 October 1857.

Left: 3. A black silk dress of 1829–30. It has been cobbled together from two other dresses, apparently in a hurry as the stitching is quite crude, and dyed black, possibly for mourning wear. The dyes are now beginning to fade differentially.

Below left: 3a. Detail of the hem, showing the careless puckering and tucks under the applied rouleaux.

Below right: 3b. Detail of the inside of the hem showing the way the fabric has been pieced and the crude stitching.

Museum collections contain a disproportionate number of 'best' dresses – wedding gowns, evening wear and silk day dresses, which were mostly worn by people who were relatively well-to-do. Poor people's clothes tended to be worn until they fell to pieces, so such items are few and far between. Joseph Dare produced annual reports for the Domestic Mission. He describes shocking poverty but seldom mentions dress except in passing. For example, in 1846 he wrote that in parts of town a visitor 'will behold narrow and badly drained streets; filthy and confined courts; and their inmates, clothed in the same dress all the year through'. In 1852 he wrote of a young woman who refused to go into the workhouse:

> Because of the mixed company and disreputable characters … She had therefore pledged all her best clothes to purchase food, and a few days before, in the depth of winter, she said she had pulled off her flannel petticoat to pawn for a loaf of bread …'[1]

4. Clara Dare's dress, *c.* 1868.

The Mission had stocks of clothes donated by philanthropic ladies and doled them out to the destitute – but these, too, often ended up with the pawnbroker.

People a little higher up the social ladder resorted to all sorts of strategies to dress respectably; the resulting garments are just as interesting as 'posh' clothes and a few examples will be included here. However, for the most part we are dependent on pictures and photographs to show us what poorer people wore.

This book is based on the collections of dress belonging to Leicester Museums and Leicestershire Museums Service. Until 1997 these formed a single collection, which I curated between 1974 and 1987. Most of the garments have a connection with the city or county, and as such this survey is somewhat limited. However, Leicester and Leicestershire were typical of many other cities and counties. Leicestershire had its fair share of stately homes and big houses – Pigot's 1841 *Directory* lists over 200 of them. The rural economy was based on framework knitting and mining as well as agriculture, and it is also fox hunting country. The county, particularly Melton Mowbray where the Quorn, the Cottesmore and the Belvoir hunts all meet, was much visited in the winter months by aristocratic huntsmen and their families. No doubt some of the hunting ladies and the huntsmen's wives and daughters patronised local dressmakers from time to time for new clothes for the many social events in the hunting calendar.

Leicester itself was as fashionable as any other county town. From the Middle Ages on the town prospered until, by 1936, the Bureau of Statistics of the League of Nations rated it the second richest city in Europe. In the nineteenth century it became a manufacturing centre and the population increased enormously, from 17,005 in 1801 to 227,222 in 1911. Many of the local factories produced textiles and clothing – caps, elastic webbing, boots and shoes, stockings and knitwear – and in 1861, a few miles

Above: 5a. Detail of join.

Left: 5. Crinoline cage. This has been put together from two separate crinolines.

6. Detail of a drawing of the Guildhall in the 1820s by John Flower. The lady kneeling on the pavement and the maidservant with her basket are wearing working women's versions of the fashions of the day.

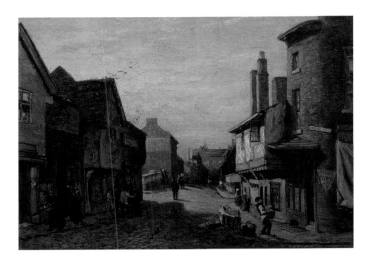

7. Detail of *Bridge Street, Leicester*, *c.* 1870, showing the dress of ordinary working people. It is by a Leicester artist, John Fulleylove (1845–1908).

8. Old people from Leicester workhouse, 1890s. Earlier in the century inmates had worn uniform, but by 1890 it seems they were allowed to wear their own clothes. Note that all the old ladies are wearing hats!

9. Child's uniform jacket from Blaby Union workhouse, Leicestershire, *c.* 1836.

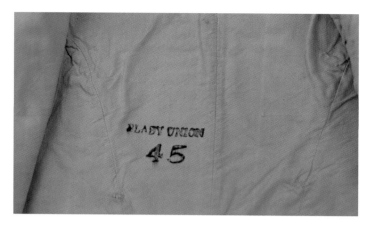

9b. Detail of the workhouse stamp on the lining. Workhouses were expected to keep a Clothing Expenditure Book in which to record 'the disposal of every article of clothing and bedding', so each item was numbered.

10. *View of Leicester*, British School, *c.* 1830. Leicester was still quite a small place – the population in 1831 was 40,639 and the countryside was still just a short walk away.

11. Stockings made by Corah of Leicester, probably for the 1862 International Exhibition. By 1855, Corah's was one of the largest hosiery firms in the country.

away in Market Harborough, the Symington brothers set up what was to become one of the UK's largest corset factories. Leicester was no backwater in terms of fashion and the museums' dress collections clearly reflect this. This study, therefore, focuses on the ladies of the city and county, with excerpts from reports in the local press and illustrations from magazines – like *Punch* and the *Girl's Own Paper* – which would have been readily available to them.

There are numerous illustrated books on dress; the aim of this one is to look at the people who made clothes and the skills they had, and at some of the people who wore those garments and how and when they wore them. It is not intended to be a chronology of the development of styles, though obviously the main fashion changes can be inferred from the illustrations.

11a. Detail of one of the stocking welts showing the date and 'NC S' for Nathaniel Corah & Son.

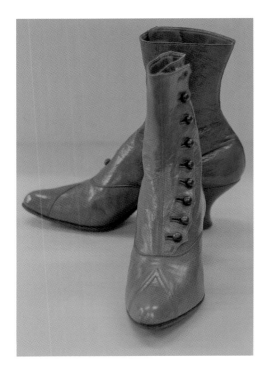

12. Pair of ladies' tan glacé leather boots. They were purchased for 16s 6d in 1896 in Leicester, but unfortunately we do not know which firm made them.

13. 'Treeing room' in an unidentified Leicester shoe factory, *c.* 1910.

Above left: 14. Corset, *c.* 1880, made by Symington's of Market Harborough.

Above right: 15. The 'Pretty Housemaid' corset, made by Symington's of Market Harborough. The design was registered in 1886. It was one of their best sellers and was intended for young working women with a little disposable income.

Chapter 1

Dressmaking and Dresses
1770–1850

Making a dress of expensive silk fabric that fits and flatters the wearer, is comfortable, well-made enough to withstand a reasonable amount of wear and tear and conforms to the latest fashion, takes a high level of skill. Dressmakers worked from pictures and fashion plates – paper patterns as we know them did not come into general use until the 1870s. Making a dress in this way requires a degree of craftsmanship, experience and understanding of materials on a par with doing fine wood carving or metalwork – though today even the finest examples seldom receive the sort of appreciation accorded to a good piece of furniture or an elaborate piece of silver. Nonetheless, for most of our period

Right: 16. Green brocade dress, 1770s. The fabric dates from the 1730s and is just 16½ inches wide with a 22-inch pattern repeat. This may well be a remake of an earlier dress, though there are no signs of earlier stitching.

Below: 16a. Detail of the bodice lining.

fabrics were of very high quality and clothes were expensive. In the eighteenth century garments were sufficiently valuable to their owners to be handed down in wills; for example, Lucy Herrick, the mother of William Herrick who built Beaumanor Hall near Leicester, died in 1778 and bequeathed her 'best black silk negligée and petticoat' to Ann Beardsley of Stoke Newington and the rest of her clothes to her daughter, Lucy Gildart.[2]

Up to the end of the seventeenth century, those women's garments that were not made at home were made by tailors, while seamstresses made items like shirts, underwear and baby linen. Gradually, women infiltrated the trade, and by the early eighteenth century

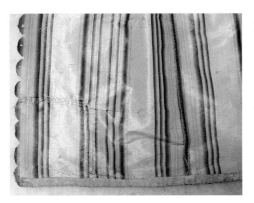

Above left: 17. Striped taffeta dress *c*. 1770–85. This was remade at least once, judging by the stitching, and has subsequently been adapted for fancy dress. It is an 'open robe' and would have been worn over a matching or contrasting 'petticoat' or underskirt.

Above right: 17a. Detail of the back. Note the way the bodice is pieced together to take account of the narrow width of the fabric.

Left: 17b. Detail of the front of the skirt. The edges have been cut with a block and pinking iron and are left raw.

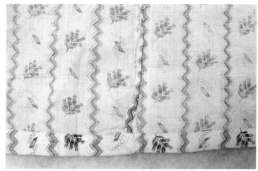

Above left: 18a. The bodice would have fastened with pins, and the skirt has an 'apron front', tying at the back with tapes.

Above right: 18b. Detail of the fabric showing the three blue lines in the selvedge, which denotes that it was made in England between 1774 and 1811. Cotton cloth woven in England carried a lower rate of excise duty when printed than cottons woven abroad.

Above left: 18. 'Round gown' (as opposed to an open robe) of roller-printed cotton, 1790s. The impractically long sleeves were meant to imply that the wearer did not do any menial work.

Above right: 19. *Mrs Martha Nichols*, painted by Francis Towne in the late 1780s. Martha Green came from Hinckley and in 1778 she married a London publisher and printer, John Nichols. She wears an open robe with matching petticoat of white fabric – it looks like cotton rather than silk – with long fitted sleeves, worn over a corset which gave her body the fashionable conical shape. She has an elaborate cap on her head, as befitted a married woman, worn over a high hairstyle.

they had created a new profession, that of 'mantua maker', or dressmaker. By the early 1800s women had an almost complete monopoly of making female clothes, though male tailors continued to make riding habits and outdoor garments.

Girls as young as nine could be apprenticed to dressmaking but the majority were in their early teens. They usually paid a 'premium' up front for the privilege of receiving training – anything up to £50, according to the type of firm for which they were working. Parish apprentices – girls from the workhouse or from poor families who were supported by the parish – would have their premium paid for them by the overseers and the standard rate for them seems to have been at the bottom of the scale, around £3. The length of apprenticeships varied; some girls served the traditional seven-year term, though as the nineteenth century progressed shorter apprenticeships became more common. Ambitious young women would then move on to becoming 'improvers' – effectively senior apprentices. They were still learning their trade and were paid pocket money, if they were paid at all. Only up-market firms employed improvers, usually in 'the season'. Then, after several years, and probably by then in her early twenties, a young woman would become an assistant dressmaker – a 'second hand' or 'third hand' depending on the size of the firm for which she worked, paid, on average, 8 to 12 shillings a week.

Above left: 20. Dressmaker's shop from *The Book of Trades*, 1811.

Above right: 21. Draper's shop from *The Book of Trades*, 1811.

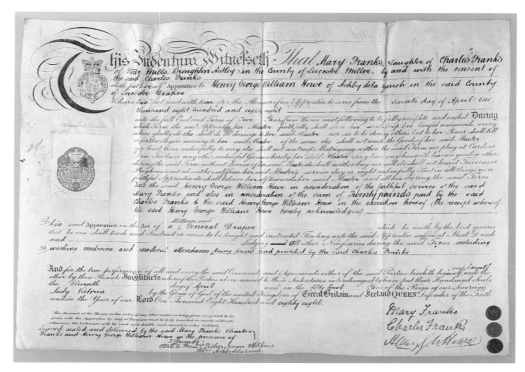

22. Apprenticeship indenture for Mary Franks, the daughter of the miller in Broughton Astley. She was apprenticed to Henry George William Howe of Ashby-de-la-Zouch, draper and milliner, for a period of two years, on 7 April 1888, and her father paid a premium of £20.

Many women never progressed beyond this stage. They married, had families, maybe returning to work when their children were grown or the family needed extra money. Their level of expertise varied, but most had learned to sew neatly, to make beautiful button holes and assemble garments cut out for them, but they had never fitted clients or learned how to make a pattern. Comparatively few women moved up the career ladder to become 'first hands' – who supervised the workroom, measured clients, drafted patterns, cut them out and advised customers on buttons and trimmings. If they could build up some savings, or were able to borrow money, these women might then set up in business on their own account, alone or in partnership with friends or relatives.

Dressmaking was a precarious trade, however. It was one of the few occupations open to girls from 'respectable' families and the trade was over-subscribed. Nineteenth-century novelists would have us believe that many dressmakers were the daughters of gentlemen fallen on hard times, but a survey of the census suggests this was seldom the case; girls who became dressmakers were usually the daughters, sisters or wives of shopkeepers and small tradesmen rather than of impoverished gentlefolk.

The profit margin on making a dress was small. In the nineteenth century, the average price for making-up ranged from 3s to 10s 6d, though a court dressmaker in London could charge considerably more. Dressmakers might make a penny or two extra on fabric and sundries they provided themselves, but after they had paid their staff, paid for fuel and lighting, rent and food, their profits were minimal. It took a good head for business to work out when to let staff go because they were costing more than they were bringing in, when and whether to turn orders away, how much time to spend on doing repairs and alterations (which customers appreciated but were time-consuming and paid less well than making garments), and just how much they could charge before customers went elsewhere. Many firms went under simply because the proprietors made the wrong calculations. Of the eighty-three firms listed in Slater's 1847 Leicester *Directory*, for example, only twenty-five were still there in 1850.

Many provincial milliners and dressmakers visited London once or twice a year and came home with samples of fabric and trimmings, new fashions in caps and bonnets and accessories, and pictures and fashion plates which would be put on display and regular customers would be invited to their 'show'. These usually took place in spring and autumn and were often advertised in the local press. Many ladies enjoyed visiting the shows but there were conventions to be observed. For example, the arrival of the new London fashions in Mrs Gaskell's *Cranford* caused Miss Matty some problems: '[T]he thing is this,' she said, 'it is not etiquette to go till after twelve; but then, you see, all Cranford will be there, and one does not like to be too curious about dresses and trimmings and caps with all the world looking on …'

MRS PEGG
Most respectfully acquaints the Ladies of Leicester and its vicinity, that her
FASHIONS for the present season will be ready for inspection on THURSDAY,
the 21st instant, when the honour of a call will be highly esteemed.
Southgates, Leicester, Nov. 14.

Leicester Chronicle, 16 November 1822.

MILLINERY AND LACE WAREHOUSE

SUMMER FASHIONS
HIGH-STREET, LEICESTER
MRS PARTRIDGE returns her sincere thanks for the extensive patronage she has
so long been honoured with, and begs to announce to her numerous Customers
and Ladies in general, that she has just returned from the Metropolis where she
has selected a
CHOICE ASSORTMENT OF MILLINERY
From most of the first-rate Parisian Houses of Fashion

Leicester Journal, 6 May 1853.

In the days before the railways made travel relatively straightforward, a visit to the capital must have been quite a daunting prospect for a working woman, and some London firms advertised their services in provincial newspapers. For example, the *Leicester Journal* for 15 April 1836 carried an advertisement aimed at 'MILLINERS & DRESSMAKERS that are in the habit of visiting the Metropolis to select their new Patterns and Fashions, will do well previous to making their purchases to call at William's and Sowerby's, 61, Oxford Street …'

Fashions in women's dress changed rapidly. In the course of her working life, a dressmaker who started as an apprentice in her early teens and continued working into her sixties would have seen four or five major changes, each of which would have necessitated learning new techniques of cutting and fitting. The illustrations on the following pages demonstrate this. Again, there are some surprises. Most dresses, even those made of silk, were lined with what, to modern eyes, seem very coarse fabrics – heavy cottons and linens, which supported the garment and took the strain when a bodice was pulled tight over the top of the corset.

Nineteenth-century fabrics came in narrow widths. Suitings, tweeds and heavy woollens were the widest (hence the term 'broadcloth') and could come in anything up to 60-inch widths. Alpaca, cashmere and some fine woollens could be 40 inches wide, and serge and some cottons might be as wide as 32–36 inches, but no other fabrics came in anything wider than 30 inches, and silks, 'fancy materials like brochés, pekins, [and] crepe de chines [were] all very narrow, less than 27 inches'.[3] This meant that bodices were assembled from a number of small pieces and were shaped by curved seams where a modern dressmaker would use darts. Skirts were made up of numerous breadths. In the mid-nineteenth century, for example, when skirts were at their widest, 16 yards of material might go into the making of a single dress. Fabrics were also expensive.

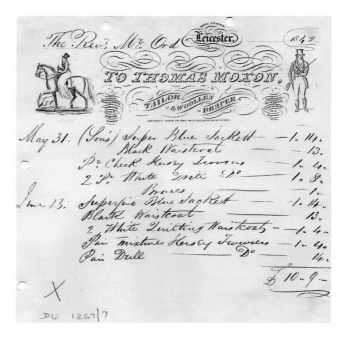

23. Billhead for Thomas Moxon, tailor. Thomas Moxon had premises on Leicester High Street and was there from the mid-1820s to the early 1860s. His billhead shows a man and a woman in clothes that were already somewhat old-fashioned when he went into business.

21

Above: 24. The Leicestershire artist John E. Ferneley and his family in his studio, 1822–3. They lived in Melton Mowbray and Ferneley specialised in painting horses and hunting scenes. His wife, daughters and younger son wear the high-waisted dresses that had been fashionable since the beginning of the century.

Left: 25. Dress of brown roller-printed lawn, *c.* 1805. The fashionable shape of the 1790s gradually became leaner and skimpier. Dresses clung to the wearer's contours and waists moved up to just below the bust.

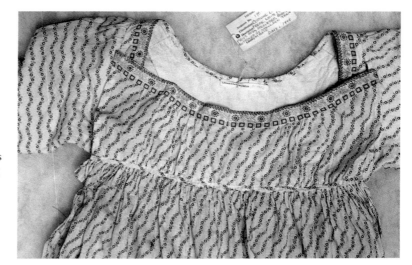

25a. The bodice has a firm cotton lining and an 'apron' front, fastening at the corners of the square neckline with loops and buttons.

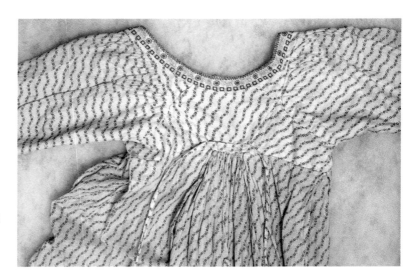

25b. The bodice back is cut in a 'diamond' shape with dropped shoulder seams and the back shaping seams curving out to the armhole

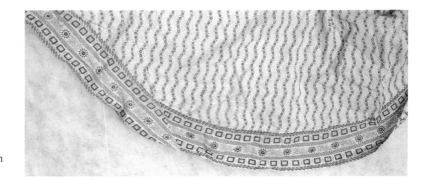

25c. The sleeves, neckline and hem are edged with a matching design in two widths.

Left: 26. Fashion plate for September 1809. Dresses of the early nineteenth century harked back to what were believed to be the 'classical' styles of Greece and Rome.

Below left: 27. Fashion plate from the *Ladies' Magazine* for September 1813. Eliza Stone would have consulted magazines like this.

Below right: 28. Fashion plate showing a ball dress for May 1827.

Right: 29. Evening dress of yellow silk with a gauze over-dress, embroidered with a design of pansies, 1820–23. High waists remained in fashion, but skirts gradually became fuller. This is a stunning dress and an example of complex dressmaking. The under-dress is of soft silk with a low round neck and puff sleeves.

Below right: 29a. The embroidery is 'tambour work' done with a fine hook through fabric stretched taut over a drum-shaped frame ('tambour' is French for drum), rather like crocheting through fabric. This is almost certainly professional work. Both the under-dress and tunic have padded rouleaux at the hems to make the skirt stand out.

Below left: 29b. Detail of the sleeve showing the elaborate shaping of the cuff and the piped edging.

Silks and woollens could cost up to a guinea a yard, though the majority were in the 2*s* 6*d* to 10*s* range. A customer who did not read her bill carefully could have been forgiven for thinking her dressmaker was making a significant amount of money.

However, the greatest problem most dressmakers faced was the long hours they had to work. Ladies were led to expect that garments could be produced in a matter of hours, and dressmakers regularly worked 12 or 14-hour days, or all night when an order required it.

In 1843 the Children's Employment Commission reported on conditions in the dressmaking trade. They interviewed young workers, forewomen, employers, local clergymen, doctors and schoolteachers. The result was a litany of shocking complaints about low pay, long hours and exploitative employers. The commissioners' powers were limited and they could only report on those firms that allowed them to visit – in Leicester they went to just three firms out of 150 – so if anything their report probably *under*estimates how bad conditions were.

Above: 30a. Detail of the 'diamond' back with piped seams. The piping prevented hand-stitched seams from gaping.

Left: 30. Dress of roller-printed muslin, *c.* 1835. The fabric is 31 inches wide and the finely detailed pattern is very typical of the 1830s. The cut is fashionable with enormously full sleeves and a full skirt.

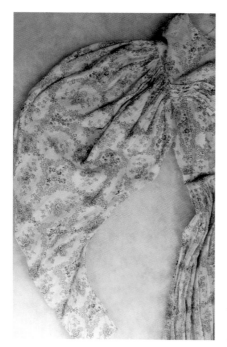

30b. Detail of the sleeve. Sleeves at this date were enormously full – known, for obvious reasons, as 'imbecile' sleeves – and were worn over padded 'sleeve muffs' or little frames.

31. Portrait of Charlotte Jane Cope, *c.* 1830, in evening dress. She was a widow in her sixties when this was painted and lived at Leamington Priors in Warwickshire.

32. Mrs William Scott. She is wearing a dress with the huge sleeves that were fashionable in the early 1830s. The portrait is said to have been painted by her son, William Wallace Scott. However, he was born in 1820, so it seems more likely that it was painted by her husband, William Scott, who was also a portrait painter.

Above: 33a. Inside of the dress showing how the skirt is folded over at the top, gathered and over-sewn to the bodice. The skirt of this dress is made up of seven breadths of 18-inch-wide silk.

Left: 33. Dress of olive green silk, *c.* 1840. By 1840, fashions had changed; the full sleeves had been replaced by tight-fitting ones, waists were much lower, often coming to a point at the front, and necklines were high and demure.

34. A young lady wearing a dress very similar to the one shown above. It is accessorised with muslin and lace under-sleeves, a net frill at the neck with a big blue and white checked bow and a black velvet ribbon and ornament – a slightly odd combination to modern eyes.

Chapter 2

Dressmaking and Dresses 1850–1914

Writers and artists drew on the 1843 report to produce novels and artworks highlighting the appalling conditions in which dressmakers worked. Mrs Elizabeth Stone's novel, *The Young Milliners*, was published in 1843 'in an attempt to awaken attention to the miseries which a great number of people … endure in their exertions to gain their daily bread, viz., the Milliner's Apprentice, and other Needleworkers …' and the author acknowledged it was based on the report's findings. Other novelists also drew on it – the best known examples are probably Mrs Gaskell's *Mary Barton* (1848) and *Ruth* (1853).

Thomas Hood's poem 'Song of the Shirt' stemmed from the same source and was first published in *Punch* in December 1843. It began:

> With fingers weary and worn,
> With eyelids heavy and red,
> A woman sat, in unwomanly rags,
> Plying her needle and thread —
> Stitch! stitch! stitch!
> In poverty, hunger, and dirt,
> And still with a voice of dolorous pitch
> She sang the 'Song of the Shirt.'

It continued in the same vein for twelve lugubrious verses.

Artists, too, produced work to tug at the viewer's heartstrings. Richard Redgrave, Anna Blunden, George Frederick Watts, George Elgar Hicks, Frank Holl, John Everard Millais and many others painted pictures of exhausted needlewomen toiling in bare attic rooms – but they are obviously posed pictures. The subjects are usually attractive young women who all appear to be quite healthy, and most of them were actually depicted as seamstresses rather than dressmakers. By the mid-nineteenth century the term 'seamstress' referred to women who worked as outworkers for drapers or wholesalers, assembling ready-cut items. Such work was even more badly paid than dressmaking.

Art and fiction are probably not the best ways of publicising real life abuses and they had little effect. Most ladies seem to have been loath to believe that their own dressmaker, someone they liked and trusted, was capable of ill-treating her staff – and

35. *The Seamstress* by Richard Redgrave, mid-1840s. He wrote that, 'It is one of my most gratifying feelings, that many of my best efforts in art have aimed at calling attention to the trials and struggles of the poor and oppressed ...'

VETO.

"SHALL WE—A—SIT DOWN?"   "I SHOULD LIKE TO; BUT MY DRESSMAKER SAYS I MUSTN'T!"

36. *Punch*, 26 February 1876.

of course, the dressmaker herself would have been quick to deny any suggestion that she might overwork her employees.

The Children's Employment Commission reported on the dressmaking trade for a second time in 1864 and found that in fact working conditions had improved very little in twenty years. London houses still regularly worked 14 to 16-hour days in the season and most provincial firms worked 12-hour days. Some employers were critical of improvements. Mrs Gregory in Cheltenham told the commissioners that when she was an apprentice, forty years previously, she had sometimes 'in an emergency' gone a week without going to bed, but said, 'Now the girls complain if they have to work through one night. I think they are either much less strong than they used to be or much more idle!'

There was, however, one major development between 1843 and 1864 that had a major impact on the dressmaking trade: the invention of the sewing machine.

From the late eighteenth century on there had been numerous attempts to produce a sewing machine but none of them worked very well. Elias Howe in America is credited with the invention of the first viable machine and various inventors added modifications. The first advertisements for sewing machines appeared in the Leicester press in October 1856. These were for a sewing machine made by W. F. Thomas, the London corsetry manufacturer who had bought Elias Howe's patent. For some years Thomas guarded this patent jealously, but by the 1860s there were a number of machines on sale made by Singer, Wilcox & Gibbs, Grover & Baker and numerous others; their price had dropped to around £6 and they could often be paid for in instalments.

W. F. THOMAS AND Co.'s
PATENT SEWING MACHINES.
PRICE FROM £15.

Advertisements like this appeared in the provincial press throughout the late 1850s.

There was some concern that treadling a machine was bad for women's reproductive organs – the combination of women and machinery was very troubling to many Victorian men – but the amount of time and effort the machines saved meant that they were soon in use in most dressmaking establishments. In the 1990s I did a survey of the dresses in what was then the Leicestershire Museums collection: of twenty-seven 1850s dresses, eight were partly or wholly machine-sewn; of thirty-three 1860s dresses, twenty-five were machine-made; of twenty-nine 1870s dresses, twenty-four were machine-stitched. However, early machines were surprisingly tiny and had their limitations. To begin with, the trickier jobs – setting in sleeves or stitching flimsy fabrics that might pucker or tear – were often still done by hand. The first machines created a chain-stitch, which would unravel if the final stitch was not secured by hand; fairly soon they were replaced by lock-stitch machines, which used interlocking upper and lower threads (like contemporary machines), but firms that had been ahead of the curve and shelled out for one of the early chain-stitch machines were unwilling to incur further expense and carried on using them well into the 1870s.

Above: 37a. Detail of a flounce showing the embroidery.

Left: 37. Dress of white tambour-embroidered muslin, early 1850s. It was worn by Sarah Ansell, who married Josiah Gimson, a Leicester engineer, in 1858. She was the mother of Ernest Gimson, the architect and furniture maker.

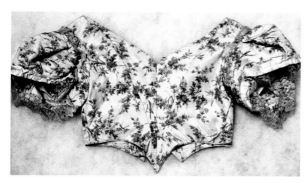

Above: 39. Front view of the bodice of an evening dress of warp-printed silk, late 1850s.

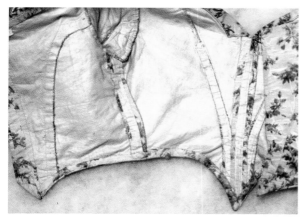

Above left: 39a. An inside view. It is beautifully made, lined with strong white cotton and boned, and entirely hand-stitched.

Above right: 39b. The skirt, shown on a hanger. It appears to have been remade in the 1890s. The full skirts of the mid-nineteenth century contained yards of fabric and so were easy to alter. The skirt seams are machine stitched and two machines – one a lock stitch, one a chain stitch – have been used, which suggests it was probably altered twice.

The introduction of machines affected the design of dresses. Mrs Gilling, a dressmaker at Promenade Villas in Cheltenham, told the commissioners she had three machines and was delighted with them, claiming that, 'Much more work can be put in too, we should never put 100 yards of trimming in a summer dress if it were all to be done by hand.'

Soon there was another type of machine on the market that also had a significant effect on design: the kilting machine, which made pleats. These began to appear in the 1870s and were quite small; they pleated strips of fabric, not whole skirts, with the result that many dresses of the 1870s and '80s had pleated decoration at the cuffs, at the hem, at the neck, decorating the skirt and so on. To begin with dressmakers sent off

38. Sarah Symington, née Gold, and her husband, James, *c.* 1850. They started a drapery business in Market Harborough in 1840. In the hands of their two eldest sons, Robert and William, Symingtons became one of the largest corset manufacturing firms in the country. Sarah wears a fashionable silk dress with wide bell-shaped sleeves and three tiers of flounces. She is still quite slim, though by the time this photograph was taken she had had at least eight of her ten children.

Left: 40. Dress of blue and green striped silk, *c.* 1865–7. This is a typical example of how dressmakers adapted the fashionable style of the 1860s by adding 'back interest', in this case in the form of a separate 'tablier'.

Below: 40a. The tablier.

 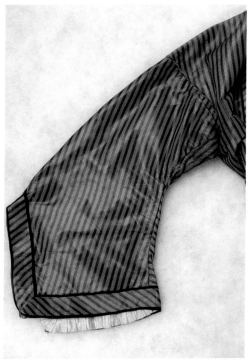

Above left: 41. Dress of brown and black striped silk, *c.* 1868. This is very similar to the previous dress but is an example of a garment made in the latest style rather than adapted to it. This dress is machine-made but the sleeves are set in by hand.

Above right: 41a. Detail showing the cut of the sleeve. For much of the mid-century sleeves were cut curved, with little fabric to spare at the elbow or shoulder, making movement difficult.

fabric to specialist firms, paying by the yard for strips of different widths with different sizes and configurations of pleats, but fairly soon the machines became so cheap that many dressmakers invested in one of their own.

Gradually, conditions in the dressmaking trade did begin to improve. The Workshop Regulation Act came into force on 1 January 1868 and regulated working hours for women and girls in line with the Factory Acts passed a few years previously. In August that year the *Leicester Journal* warned:

> It is well that employers should know that, under the Workshops Regulation Act, no young women employed as milliners, etc. may be kept at work after 2 o'clock on Saturday afternoon. For infringing this law, a shopkeeper named Roebuck, at Blackburn, was fined on Wednesday.

There were comparatively few such prosecutions, the fines levied were relatively small and the law was frequently bent and broken, but little by little dressmakers' hours did get shorter.

Above left: 42. Wedding dress of grey and lilac silk, *c.* 1875. The bride who wore this was probably in the later stages of mourning – these were 'half-mourning' colours. This dress is most beautifully cut and stitched using a lock-stitch machine.

Above right: 42a. View of the back.

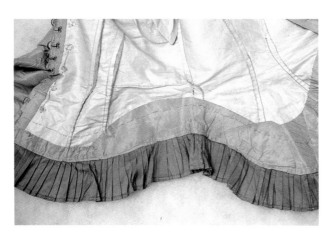

42b. Detail of the inside of the bodice.

Right: 43. Fashion plate from the *Dressmaker and Warehouseman's Gazette* showing dresses with kilted trimmings. Undated, but mid-1870s.

Below left: 44. Gold satin dress, *c*. 1886. This dress was made by Mrs Blakesley of 56, King Street, Leicester – her name and address are woven into the petersham waistband. The dress is bulky and heavy and not particularly well-made.

Below right: 44a. Back view.

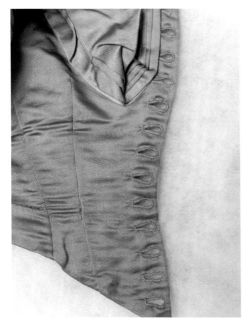

Above: 44b. Detail showing the waist band.

Left: 44c. Detail of buttonholes.

There were other factors too. Between 1850 and 1870 many drapers' shops developed into what we would now call 'department stores'. Leicester had several – including Adderly's on the Market Place and Morgan and Squire's on Hotel Street, which were both established by 1861. Joseph Johnson's (in the building which became Fenwick's) arrived a few years later, and Gee Nephew on Gallowtree Gate was set up in around 1890. Isabel Ellis (née Evans) remembered the Leicester of her childhood:

> I well remember Adderly's about 1870 as the largest and most beautiful shop in Leicester. It may have been a quarter of its present [1935] size … I had gone to Leicester with my mother and she was buying grown-up clothes. After standing by her till I was bored, I pulled her sleeve and said couldn't I have some stuff to make a frock for my doll. The assistant overheard, and, with great politeness inquired if the young lady would care to have some patterns of fringes and buttons. He promptly produced a boxful of these … My mother did not buy for me the six inches of pale-blue velvet, cut on the cross, for which I begged; but I was too entranced by bits of rainbow-hued fringe to think any more of it … Another very superior shop in Leicester was Morgan and Squire's in Hotel Street – a single shop at the corner of Friar Lane, where our mother bought excellent house-linen and tea-towels, and was waited on by a deferential gentleman with a bald head, who said, 'This is the quality you like, Madam.'[4]

Service was service in the nineteenth century! Many of the stores opened departments for dressmaking, tailoring and upholstery, providing equally excellent service.

Soon, training in a department store workroom became the aim of most would-be dressmakers. Private dressmakers had long been accused of not teaching their apprentices properly, keeping them as unpaid labour to do boring, time-consuming jobs like stitching long straight seams, turning up hems and making button-holes, and not teaching them how to cut and fit for fear that an able apprentice might go off and set up a business in opposition to their own. The department store owners had no such fears and it was in their interests to train up as many competent hands as possible. Not only did they not charge an apprentice premium, they could attract ambitious girls from far afield because they had their own boarding houses for staff and were known to take a paternalistic interest in their employees' welfare – an important consideration for the parents of girls moving away from home to work.

In addition, technical colleges began to offer training courses for milliners and dressmakers, enabling them to go into the trade without serving lengthy apprenticeships. From being a trade that exploited and overworked its members, by the 1880s and '90s the dressmaking and millinery trades were being recast as careers-with-prospects for ambitious young women – even though, for many, conditions had not changed radically since 1864. Dressmaking was now being described as a science – Leicester even had one firm that styled itself the 'Scientific Dresscutting Establishment', though whether it had any links to the establishment of the same name in London's Regent Street is not clear.

Alongside these developments in training, from the 1870s on a whole industry developed supplying purpose-printed paper patterns, dressmakers' dummies, instruction manuals, new systems of cutting and measuring, waistbands that could have the firm's name woven into them and a host of other new goods and services.

Right: 45. Dress of red corded silk trimmed with red silk net, *c.* 1885, made by the 'Scientific Dress-cutting Establishment, Leamington House, Market Street, Leicester'. In fact there is nothing particularly unusual about the cut.

Below: 45a. Detail of the waistband.

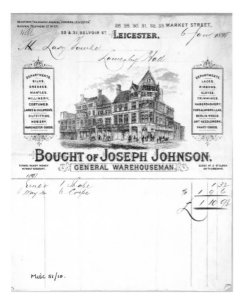

Left: 46. Bill from Joseph Johnson's department store, dated January 1898.

Below: 47. Advertisement for the French Bust Company on Tottenham Court Road. These advertisements appeared regularly in the *Draper's Record*, a trade journal, in 1895.

Above left: 48. Purple dress of ribbed silk, *c.* 1895. This was made by Adderly's of Leicester for a Mrs Cooper. The dress looks deceptively simple, but in fact it is very cleverly designed and extremely well-made. The bodice fastens with alternating rows of hooks and eyes. The sleeves are fashionably full on the shoulders, though the lining fits closely all the way up the arm. The fullness is created by clever cutting and pleating – there is no additional piecing to create the shape.

Above right: 48b. Back view.

48a. Inside of the bodice showing the lining, the beautifully scalloped seams, the boning and Adderly's label.

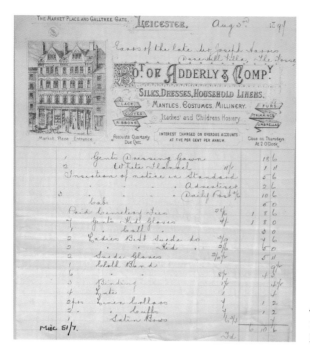

49. Adderly's billhead dated August 1897, showing their shop on Leicester Market Place.

CRUELLE ENIGME; OR, TWOS INTO ONE WON'T GO.

THE PROBLEM OF THE DAY:—HOW TO GET THIS YEAR'S SLEEVES INTO LAST YEAR'S JACKET.

50. *Punch* cartoon, 18 November 1893, lampooning the fashion for very full sleeves.

51. Two views of the bodice of a pink silk dinner dress, trimmed with velvet and machine-made lace, mid-1890s.

52. Photo of Priscilla Wiggins, *c.* 1900. She was a widow in her sixties, and in 1901 she was living on West Bridge Street with her three unmarried children, keeping a grocer's shop and selling beer. She is smartly dressed in black silk.

Chapter 3

Dresses and the People Who Wore Them

For the most part, our forebears had fewer clothes than we do. Women wore dresses, accessorised with shawls and fichus, collars and cuffs, laces, ribbons and jewellery, but they did not have the range of mix and match separates with which we are familiar today.

We have some information about how one young Leicestershire woman dressed in the early years of the century. She was Eliza Stone. Her father had the tenancy of a farm in Knighton owned by Sir Edward Hartopp, and he also valued land and collected rents for various noblemen and gentlemen, including the Duke of Rutland at Belvoir and Lord Lanesborough at Swithland. In Eliza's childhood, Knighton was a small village with about 300 inhabitants, and Eliza described the family home as the 'only substantial house' there apart from Knighton Hall, where Sir Edward spent some of his time. Eliza was one of nine children. She and her three elder sisters were sent to school in Mansfield in Nottinghamshire but came home in 1807 when Eliza was ten; their education continued with a series of French, mathematics and drawing masters who visited the family home. She and her sisters also did some work that sounds quite menial, but was presumably thought appropriate for a gentleman farmer's daughters. 'We used to plait straw and have it made up for our hats. It was sold in bundles ready for splitting and plaiting. It was nice work, and pillow lace I liked making, but I did not like spinning so well,' she remembered, though she went on to say that her mother and sister Harriet had 'pretty little spinning wheels' for 'their own amusement'. In 1813, when she was sixteen, Eliza began to keep a diary in which she recorded her expenditure.

Her parents were quite generous – she had a quarterly allowance of £1 15s plus 2s 2d in cash, and with small gifts and payments 'per lavora' (helping in the house) she had an income of around £16 a year, most of which she spent on clothes. In that first year she seems to have been kitting herself out for her almost-adult life. She bought:

Pelisse (a type of light coat)	£4 0s 0d
White muslin for a frock	10s 3d
Batella* for a frock	8s 0d
Batella dress	10s 6d
Another	10s 4d
Batella gown	11s 11d

Leno frock	9s 0d
Red frock	17s 0d
Batella for a spencer (a short jacket)	1s 11½d
'Yellow ribband and sarsnet' for a 'body'	2s 6d
Eleven pairs of gloves	
Pair of boots	12s 0d
Coloured boots	8s 6d
Six pairs of shoes, including ones in white satin, black kid, sealskin and lemon kid	
Four chemises	£1 1s 0d
Calico for two nightgowns	9s 6d
Pink handkerchief	3s 0d
Green veil	3s 3d
Parasol	£1 1s 0d
White necklace	6s 0d
Petticoat	6s 1½d
Bonnet	10s 0d
Another	10s 7d

* 'Batella' was a fine cotton fabric.

She also acquired a tooth brush, a tooth comb, had her hair cut each month, got her boots, shoes, stays and a brooch mended, had feathers curled, silk stockings re-footed and a petticoat glazed. The rest of her money went on ribbons, sashes, shoe bows, flowers, collars, handkerchiefs and the like. Sometimes she mentions what the trimmings were for, so we learn that she already had in her wardrobe a grey dress, a pink frock, a green frock and at least two bonnets.

Her total expenditure in 1813 was £21 5s 9d – more than her recorded income so perhaps she had some savings – of which all but £2 0s 3d was spent on dress or related items. Fashionable boots and shoes were very flimsy at this date, and a lady always wore gloves outside the home, hence the number of those items. No payments are recorded to dressmakers so Eliza probably made some of her own clothes, though by 1820 she was patronising Mrs Pegg, one of whose advertisements appears on page 20. The accounts continue until 1835, by which time Eliza was married, but she never again spent so much in a single year; in 1830, for example, she spent just £6 4s 8d.

Years later, in her memoir, she described how she had dressed as a girl.

We girls always wore coloured prints in the morning and put on white when we dressed for the 3 o'clock dinner. Short sleeves were sometimes worn with the morning dress, but more frequently long sleeves. A 'Spencer' [short jacket] was put on for going out. Waists were very short, and skirts were short too so as to show the sandal which crossed the instep and then was brought round and tied in a bow. We varied our white dresses by having different coloured ribbons, sometimes sashes, sometimes braces, and in other fanciful ways.[5]

Eliza came from a well-to-do family but by modern standards her wardrobe was still quite small. People in the past had fewer clothes partly because many fabrics were of a higher quality than we see today, so garments lasted longer and could be altered

Above: 54. Black satin shoes, *c*. 1820. These are indoor shoes, but outdoor shoes were often equally flimsy, which is why young Eliza Stone bought so many pairs.

Left: 53. Knighton, from a drawing by the Leicester artist John Flower, made in February 1836. This is the Knighton Eliza Stone (later Spurrett) would have known.

and remade as fashion changed, and partly because throughout the eighteenth and nineteenth centuries clothes were comparatively costly. For example, Joseph Moxon of Market Bosworth earned £200 a year as steward and rent collector to the Dixie family, and supplemented this by income from a small farm. He was comfortably well off, but not by any means rich. In April 1798 he spent £1 4*s* on 'A new gown – wife' and 4*s* 6*d* on 'Cambric for frills' – cambric is fine white linen and the frills were probably to go with the dress. However, these appear to be the only items of dress he bought for his wife in the two years covered by the diary.[6]

For the poor, clothing was a major expense. For example, in the nineteenth century a pair of men's boots cost more than many labourers earned in a week, and if a working man's wife ever had a new print dress made it would have cost her around 10*s* – more than double a week's rent on a cottage or terraced house.

Not only were clothes expensive, there was little room for originality. When, for example, fashion decreed that skirts be worn over a crinoline, that was what any fashion-conscious female – mistress and maidservant alike – had to wear, regardless of how impractical it was. In fact crinolines were downright dangerous. By 1858 they were becoming very large and at the end of February that year the *Leicester Journal* printed an article entitled 'DEATH IN THE HOOP OR THE FATAL PETTICOAT' announcing that in the first seven weeks of the year no fewer than fourteen ladies had died when their crinolines caught fire. 'Wood fires,' the article claimed, 'which are laid upon the hearth are the most dangerous, and the flame from them rises in an instant.' Four years later, the Sheffield coroner estimated that he was doing on average two autopsies a month on ladies who had burnt to death in their crinolines[7], and week after week the Leicester press reported terrible accidents from all across the country. In Leicester itself, young Elizabeth Woodward, visiting her sister in Duke Street, fell victim. She rushed out into the street with her dress ablaze, no doubt fanning the flames as she ran, and was rescued by a young man who smothered the flames with a blanket. She was taken to hospital, but died two months later of her burns.[8]

Crinolines were a menace in other ways too. In May 1857 a toddler was swept off Wellington Bridge in Dover by two ladies rustling past in crinolines, according to the *Leicester Mercury*, but fortunately was rescued from the water frightened but unharmed; in Bath a man pushing a wheelchair was knocked off the kerb and broke his foot.[9] In Southwark in January 1862 the *Leicester Journal* reported that a shopkeeper sued young Miss Wilson whose crinoline had knocked over a cleaner's ladder and broken his shop window. There were many such accidents. Smugglers and thieves used their crinolines to hide contraband and stolen goods. Ladies caused delays at turnstiles and monopolised the pavements – in Boston, Massachusetts, a young woman was actually fined for 'obstructing the sidewalk'.[10] Crinoline wearers also got stuck in narrow spaces; in Leicester, the gap between the posts at the end of New Walk, a fashionable tree-lined promenade, had to be widened to allow ladies to pass through.[11] Working women were especially at risk, particularly those working in factories or as cooks in kitchens. A particularly dreadful example was reported in the *Leicester Mercury* for 7 July 1860. Seventeen-year-old Sarah Ann Murfin, an employee at Wright, Holdsworth & Company's factory in Sheffield, got her crinoline entangled in a drive shaft and was dragged into the machinery: 'The girl was dead when released, her skull being dreadfully fractured, one leg nearly torn off, and her body otherwise shockingly injured.' Ironically, Wright & Holdsworth's manufactured steel wire for crinoline frames.

Nonetheless, despite the deaths and injuries and the mockery of cartoonists and the press in general, crinolines continued to be worn, with slight changes of shape, up to 1870. They were flattering to most figures, gave the wearer a good deal of personal space and, because they kept the skirts away from the legs and feet, they were easy to walk in.

Crinolines were followed by equally risible, but slightly less dangerous fashions – the crinolette and the bustle. By 1870 the vogue for dresses with 'back interest' verged on the ridiculous, making their wearers appear almost deformed. The fashionable shape was dubbed 'the Grecian bend' and was complemented by a fashion for wearing enormous chignons of – usually false – hair. The fashion is mentioned in the Irish song 'Where the Praties (potatoes) Grow':

She was just the sort of creature
That nature did intend
To walk throughout the world, my boys
Without the Grecian Bend,

Nor did she wear the chignon,
I'd have ye all to know
And I met her in the garden
Where the praties grow …

COOL REQUEST.

Lady Crinoline. " You won't mind Riding on the Box, Edward dear, will you?—I'm afraid, if we both go inside the Brougham, my New Dress will get so rumpled!"

55. *Punch* cartoon, 31 January 1857. Crinolines took up an enormous amount of space.

DINING UNDER DIFFICULTIES.

56. *Punch* cartoon, 3 November 1860. Another comment on the size of crinolines.

57. Fashion plate of 1860. Skirts were at their widest in the early 1860s.

Above left: 58. Dress of bright blue silk and ecru glazed embroidered cotton, early 1870s. This is an extremely elaborate two-piece dress, and came with a matching collar and a small cape shaped to fit over the bustle.

Above right: 59. Sheet music, *c.* 1870.

60. Mrs Priscilla Bark, *c*. 1870. She was in her fifties when this photograph was taken. She had been a milliner with premises on Leicester's Granby Street, but by 1871 she had retired and moved to De Montfort Street.

Left: 61. Crinolette, early 1870s. This succeeded the crinoline and gave the fashionable shape seen in the preceding pictures.

Below: 62. After the crinolette came the bustle. Many were home-made – a simple pad on a waistband – but this one was commercially produced and is made of 'American braided wire'.

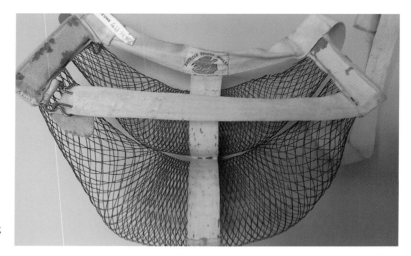

62a. Detail showing the label.

"CHACUN POUR SOI."

Lady's-Maid. "I BEG PARDON, MA'AM, BUT YOUR DRESS IS TRAILING—HADN'T I BETTER LOOP IT UP BEFORE YOU GO OUT?"

Lady. "NO, THANKS, PARKER, I PREFER LETTING IT TRAIL, AS IT'S THE FASHION JUST NOW——"

Lady's-Maid. "YES, MA'AM—BUT AS THE DRESS IS TO BE *MINE* SOME DAY, I THINK *I* OUGHT TO HAVE SOME SAY IN THE MATTER!"

63. *Punch*, 4 November 1876. It was common practice for ladies to pass on their outworn clothing to their maids.

Failure to follow the dictates of fashion was something only the very rich, the very poor or the very eccentric dared to do. For anyone else it would have been social suicide. For example, in the early 1840s Mary Linwood, the famous Leicester embroideress, immortalised by Dickens and admired by Queen Victoria, appeared at a display of dancing at the Leicester Assembly Rooms, put on by pupils from the school she had founded. Young Mary Kirby attended the event and years later saw fit to poke gentle fun at the old lady who wore 'a wig of jet black curls, and a neck of wax, slightly concealed by nets and ribbons and laces'.[12] Miss Linwood was nearly ninety and was wearing accessories that were twenty years out of date. Her celebrity status allowed her to get away with it.

In *How to Dress Well on a Shilling a Day* (or £15 a year), published in 1876, 'Sylvia' described what we would call a 'capsule' wardrobe for her readers. She assumed that they would not be starting from scratch; they would already have a stock of underwear, collars, cuffs, laces and so on. It would, she advised, cost about 30s a year to keep this stock in repair and replace items as they wore out. A further £3 a year was to be set aside for boots and shoes, and £1 for gloves (eight pairs at 2s 6d each plus 1s 6d for cleaning them). Gloves were as important a part of a woman's wardrobe in the 1870s as they had been for Eliza Stone in 1813. This left £9 8s 6d for dresses, bonnets and mantles. As a bare minimum, she suggested ladies should have one hat and one bonnet for winter and one of each for summer, at a suggested price of 13s or 14s apiece, though they need not be replaced every year. She strongly recommended her readers to learn how to make or trim their own headgear, and advised them against using cheap feathers, which soon looked tatty. Hats and bonnets were supposed to match the dresses they were worn with, and, to reduce expense, Sylvia recommended that her readers keep to a single colour range in their choice of clothes – she suggested brown. Respectable ladies did not wear bright colours, according to Sylvia, and she argued that garments that had to 'do' for several seasons 'should not call attention to themselves'.

No allowance was made for paying the dressmaker – Sylvia's ladies were expected to make their own clothes, and in case they could not she included basic instructions – but she did suggest that they should spend £2 a year on a jacket 'from the tailor if possible', one for winter and one for summer, to be purchased in alternate years. The basic wardrobe would consist of a brown cashmere dress, one good quality black grenadine (a light, open-weave figured silk), 'which must be respectfully regarded for out of £15 a year how are we ever to have another?', a white piqué (a crisp cotton), a striped lawn, two or three muslins and two or three thick morning dresses, an everyday dress for church and visiting and a simple dress for evening parties and dinners:

It is a good idea to wear black very often for dinner, if dressing for that meal be the rule. Black grenadine is invaluable in this way. Like silk, it will 'do up' over and over again, and, worn with different coloured ribbons, one does not get tired of it … summer muslins with pretty fichus will also do for dinner.

Isabel Ellis's mother would have agreed with her:

Ladies of my mother's station did not accumulate evening dresses. A 'black silk' that would stand alone, worn with a real lace fichu, would go through many editions, and we all thought it quite stately.

Most of the rest of Sylvia's £15 was to be spent on trimmings to revamp dresses and bonnets, and on wraps and fichus to give familiar dresses a new lease of life, but a pound or two was to be kept in hand in case an unexpected invitation made a new outfit essential. She was full of advice about buying good-quality fabrics, cleaning garments, adding coloured neckties to basic (brown) dresses to brighten them up and re-trimming hats and bonnets. 'Poverty must, above all, not have the appearance of poverty', she stressed. If everyone who read her book had taken her advice, Sylvia would have put many a dressmaker out of business!

No doubt some women had more dresses and some had fewer than Sylvia recommended, but surviving accounts suggest that, broadly speaking, her suggestions reflected reality, at least for her middle class readers. However, Mrs Louisa Booth, the highly respectable wife of a Birmingham brass founder, remembered that in the 1860s:

> Grown-up girls would possess three dresses, distinguished as 'hightem, tightem and scrub'; two hats, for best and everyday; white cotton stockings for usual wear, and – if they were fortunate – one or two pairs of silk stockings for balls. Underclothing (we never talked of undies) was made of 'longcloth', meaning serviceable white calico, trimmed with tucks and white embroidery; red flannel petticoats were a matter of course.[13]

By 'grown-up girls' she probably meant girls in their late teens – married women were probably rather better provided for – but even so, Louisa's family seems to have been unusually parsimonious.

Working women had even fewer clothes. Ada Jackson came from a 'respectable' working class family: her father was an elastic web weaver, her mother a housewife, and Ada was an only child. The family lived comfortably but modestly in a terraced house in Leicester's Pares Street, near the town centre. In 1883, when she was nineteen, Ada began to keep a diary, detailing the minutiae of her everyday existence at home and at work.[14] She was a machinist at Thomas Webster & Company's hat and cap factory in East Bond Street, though the work was not regular and she was often laid off for a day or half-day's 'holiday'. She was paid piece-work rates and recorded her 'highest ever' week's earnings on 1 December 1883 as 13s 8d, though many weeks she earned far less and no doubt much of her wage went to her mother for her keep.

Ada was as interested in clothes as any other young woman and she also seems to have been a capable needlewoman; she records altering clothes and trimming hats for her various girlfriends. Nonetheless, in 1883 the only purchases she records are a 'round hat', a mackintosh and a 'Sunday best' dress and jacket, purchased in May from Dora Twigger, a dressmaker on Havelock Street and made by her assistant, Ada's friend, Annie Baker. She had a hat trimmed to match it, but had to go to Gee Nephews' department store, rather than the much cheaper milliner recommended by Mrs Twigger, as that lady could not do it for three weeks. 'It will cost me a pretty penny', complained Ada. However, later in the year she had another hat trimmed for just 8d.

Women had dresses for special occasions and for particular stages in life. One unusual example is the 'Quaker dress' worn by Priscilla Ellis. Her husband, John Ellis, was a rich man, a local dignitary, town councillor, a Quaker and an entrepreneur. He was prominent in the anti-slavery movement, was a social reformer, MP for Leicester from 1848 to 1852 and a director of the Midland Railway. John and Priscilla had ten children, and from 1846 the family lived at Belgrave Hall, which is now a museum.[15] It is difficult to date Priscilla's dress. From the cut it would appear to date from around 1800, but Priscilla was not born until 1798, so it must be at least twenty years later than that. The Quakers did not have a uniform as such but they were encouraged to dress plainly and not to follow the dictates of fashion. It seems likely that the dress was made to wear on Sundays to the Great Meeting and may have been worn for many years. It was presented to the museum along with a matching cape and sleeves, Priscilla's plain black bonnet, three indoor caps, two plain beige woollen shawls and a pair of brown kid shoes.

At least one of Priscilla's spinster daughters was rather more fashion conscious. The Miss Ellis's dressmaker was Miss Johnstone in Market Street and she recalled that 'Miss Jane' always knew exactly what she wanted, and, a devout Quaker like her mother, wore 'a great deal of dark grey'. Her sisters, Margaret and Charlotte,

> … would have all the boxes out, and look at the materials, and have a bit of beautiful stuff for the front, but always have it veiled with net. Sometimes Miss Isabella would fancy something too beautiful, and the others would say: 'Oh, that's not suitable. Wouldn't do at all' and the box would be put away. Then after they'd all gone,

Left: 64a. A 'Quaker' bonnet worn by Priscilla Ellis, probably in the 1830s.

Below: 64b. The cape and sleeves that went with the dress.

65. A photograph of Priscilla Ellis (1798–1872)
c. 1860. She wears a plain dark dress,
accessorised with a high cap of the type favoured
by Quaker ladies and a simple wool shawl.

66. A photograph of her two youngest
daughters Charlotte (1836–1917) and Ellen
(1839–1922), wearing matching dresses, 1860s.

Miss Isabella would slip back by herself and ask to look at it again. Presently she'd muster up courage and exclaim: 'I'll go for it!'[16]

While Priscilla's dress is a curiosity, wedding dresses survive in large numbers, some being kept for sentimental reasons, others worn as 'best' until they went out of fashion or would no longer fit their wearers. We are familiar with the idea that not all nineteenth-century wedding dresses were white – the idea that they should be, and that white symbolises purity, is a relatively modern concept. Wedding dresses in the nineteenth century followed the prevailing fashion; they were not a separate genre as they are today.

On 11 August, Ada Jackson and her friends Lily and Kate got talking about what they would like to wear if they got married, and Ada recorded the conversation:

Lily would like a Cream Cashmere dress, wreath and fall [veil]. Kate would like the same and a hat, I should like the same but I don't think a cream dress would suit me. I should rather like a Ruby Silk. Lily thinks a wreath and fall would suit me best as I look better without my hat.

Ada married on 29 December 1884 to her childhood sweetheart, George Beecroft. She described it as 'a wonderful happy day for me', but unfortunately does not tell us whether she wore ruby silk.

Once married, many women got pregnant quickly and had repeated pregnancies. Being 'enceinte' was a condition that most women tried to conceal for as long as possible; once their condition became obvious they were expected to stay at home – hence the term 'confinement'. Some fashions were easier than others for pregnant women to wear. The high-waisted dresses of the early nineteenth century, for example, were not dissimilar to twentieth-century maternity smocks, and the full skirts of 1830–70 hid a multitude of sins – though the dropped waists of the 1840s must have made concealment difficult and the narrow skirts of the late 1870s and '80s must have made it impossible. No wonder many women continued to lace themselves into corsets for as long as possible. Symingtons developed a maternity corset in the 1880s that let out, a little, as the pregnancy progressed. But even when confined to the home for the last month or two of their pregnancies, women had to wear something, and a very rare example of such a garment can be seen on page 59.

Something equally unusual is a nursing dress of around 1850, seen on page 60, which was worn by the wife of a farmer in the village of Anstey. Wealthy women often employed wet nurses to breastfeed their babies, or had their nannies bottle-feed the children on cows' milk or the various forms of patent baby food that were coming on to the market in the nineteenth century, but women who were less concerned about their social position still fed their own babies. This is an ingenious solution to that problem. The dress is well worn, though whether the buttoned slits were much used is open to question; they do not show the signs of stretching and tearing that one might expect.

While pregnancy and feeding babies had to be concealed, nineteenth-century society was much more accepting of death than we are today. It was more common for young people and children to die; accidents, illness and epidemics were rife and medicine was inadequate to deal with them. In terms of clothes, a whole etiquette developed about how those left behind should dress – and this outward display of grief bore most heavily

67. Dress of 'nun's veiling' and silk, 1880–1. This was almost certainly a wedding dress. Most of the garment is machine-made but the sleeves are set in by hand. The skirt is immensely heavy and is attached to a coarse webbing waistband, which is secured at the centre back by three heavy-duty hooks and eyes. The upper part of the skirt is of silk so that the hip-length bodice could slide over it neatly.

Right: 67a. Detail of the sleeve showing kilted silk trimming and lace.

Below: 67b. Detail of the hem showing the under-frill or 'balayeuse'.

68. Fashion plate, *La Mode Artistique*, August 1880, showing a similarly elaborate wedding dress.

Above left: 69. Wedding dress of soft blue silk crepe. It was worn by Sarah Anderson when she married Peter Sinclair on 8 January 1913 in Toxteth, Liverpool. He was a post office clerk. The dress follows the fashionable columnar shape, but though it looks loose and flowing, the bodice lining and sleeves are actually very tight-fitting.

Above right: 69a. The bodice back.

Above left: 70. This is an unusual garment, obviously intended to be worn by a woman in the later stages of her pregnancy or shortly after giving birth. It is said to date from around 1860 and has the fashionable full skirt of the period, but it seems unlikely that the wearer would have worn a crinoline underneath it.

Above right: 70a. The front. There are no signs of there ever having been any way of fastening the over-bodice, though the under-bodice fastens quite tightly with hooks and eyes.

Right: 71. Maternity corset, *c*. 1880, of black sateen. The laces at the sides allowed it to be let out as the pregnancy progressed.

Above: 72a. Detail of the inside of the bodice showing the slits. They show little sign of wear though the dress itself is faded and well worn.

Left: 72. Nursing dress, 1845–50. The frills on the bodice cleverly conceal two buttoned slits through which the wearer hoped to feed her baby.

on the women in the family. For a husband a woman was expected to wear black – usually bombazine, which was a matt fabric – trimmed with crepe, for a year. The amount of crepe was reduced at intervals and after a year could be discarded altogether; however, she was expected to wear black for at least another year, although jet jewellery and a white collar might be allowed. In 1840 *The Workwoman's Guide* listed the length of time she was expected to mourn other relatives:

For a parent – 6 months or a year
For children over 10 – 6 months to a year
For younger children – 3–6 months+
For infants – 6 weeks+
For brothers and sisters – 6–8 months
For uncles and aunts – 3–6 months
For cousins and uncles and aunts by marriage – 6 weeks to 3 months
For more distant relatives and friends – 3 weeks+

For friends, mourning was an optional mark of respect. In 1829 Mrs Suffield Brown of Cold Overton (near Oakham) wrote to her friend, Mrs Harrington, asking advice about what she should wear to mourn 'an affectionate neighbour and friend'. Mrs Harrington asked around among her own circle, and replied that the consensus was that she should wear 'nothing but cloth' – a rather odd phrase, which seems to have meant dresses in matt black cloth without crepe trimmings.[17] As a result of their desire to show respect to the deceased and their families, older women were seldom out of black.

It even affected brides. Young women would be expected to delay their wedding if a close relative died and, when they did marry, to have a wedding dress in 'mourning colours' – combinations of white, grey, black and lilac. The rules got more rigorous as the century progressed, partly as a result of Queen Victoria's excessive display of grief at the death of Prince Albert, but even in 1828, Eliza Stone, the farmer's daughter in Knighton, was expected to delay her wedding by a year because her father died. 'I was married in a Silk Dress and Bonnet to match, in a half-mourning colour,' she wrote in her memoirs. She married Samuel Spurrett, a 'landed proprietor', and they lived on Rutland Street in Leicester. He died in 1854 and it is the widowed Eliza we see on page 62.

As the century progressed, a whole industry developed to supply mourning to the bereaved in the shortest possible time. Specialist 'mourning warehouses' – like Harrison & Smart on Leicester Market Place – sprang up, employing dressmakers to strain their eyes stitching black fabrics with black thread, long into the night, by the light of guttering lamps and candles.

73. Mourning cape, trimmed with crepe, 1890s.

73a. Detail of the crepe trimming.

74. Eliza Spurrett, neé Stone, *c.* 1855. She is wearing crepe on her dress so she is in mourning, probably for her husband, Samuel, who died in 1854.

Chapter 4

Technology

The nineteenth century was an age of invention and technological development. Some of those inventions changed the world – railways, the telegraph, refrigeration and anaesthesia, for example – but there were many others and a significant number of them were applied to textiles and dress. Whole books have been written about some of these and the purpose of this chapter is simply to show and describe some relevant examples rather than to give a complete overview.

Roller Printing

A method of applying a coloured pattern to cloth, roller printing was invented by the Scotsman Thomas Bell in 1783 to replace the earlier technique of printing from engraved copper plates, which was slow and labour-intensive. The simplest form of a roller-printing machine consisted of a cast-iron pressure cylinder and an engraved copper

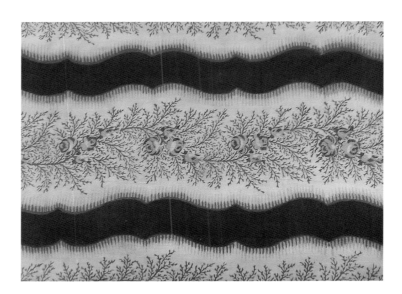

75. *Right and overleaf*: Examples of roller-printed fabrics, 1820s–1840s.

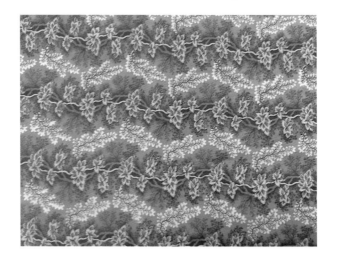

that was supplied with colour from a wooden roller that revolved in a colour-box below it. The fabric to be printed passed between the pressure cylinder and the engraved roller, which carried the dye. The pressure cylinder was wrapped in layers of cloth, and it was this slightly flexible covering that helped press the cloth to be printed into the lines of the engraving. One complete revolution of the engraved roller made up one pattern repeat. 'Doctor' blades scraped the excess dye off the engraved rollers and cleared away loose filaments and fluff. Machines could have several sets of rollers to enable them to print designs with several colours, though aligning those rollers so the different colours printed in perfect register was a complicated task.

Machine-Made Lace

Hand-made lace was a luxury item, laborious and intricate to make; in the eighteenth century a pair of lace sleeve frills could cost more than the garment they were intended to adorn. However, by the early nineteenth century various types of much cheaper, machine-made lace were available. Some laces were a form of knitting, made on machines adapted from the stocking frame – a development attributed to Robert Frost and dating from the 1760s. In 1808 John Heathcoat's twist-net machine produced net that was virtually indistinguishable from the hand-made variety, and it quickly replaced hand-made net as the ground for appliqué laces like Honiton. This was followed by the Leavers machine, invented in around 1813 in Nottinghamshire by John Levers. It was very similar to Heathcoat's machine but used much finer bobbins set closer together, which made it easier to create patterned laces. In 1828 Leavers lace machines were adapted to the Jacquard punch-card system, widening the range of designs that could be produced. Other laces were produced with embroidery machines, embroidering

76. *Right and overleaf*: Examples of various types of machine-made lace.

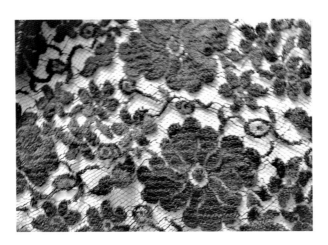

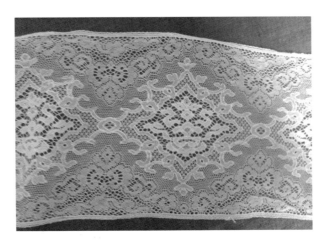

designs on to backgrounds that were then dissolved away, leaving just the pattern. This is sometimes called 'chemical' lace.

There was a certain snobbery about lace – 'Sylvia' urged her ladies to wear 'good, old lace', in other words, inherited hand-made items – but machine-made laces were ubiquitous and many people could not (and cannot) distinguish them from hand-made ones. A further confusion arises because many machine-made laces were 'hand-run'; in other words, an outline to the design was put in by hand, usually in a thick, silky thread. This was a form of outwork, particularly in Nottingham, where hundreds of women were employed as 'lace runners'.

Elastic Web

The elastic web industry in Leicester dates from 1839, when Caleb Bedells, an inventor in the hosiery firm of Wheeler & Co. of Abbey Mills, announced that he was about to commence the production of 'an improved caouchouc webbing' and opened a factory in Southgate Street. The discovery relied on the fact that treating rubber with sulphur (vulcanisation) made it resistant to heat and cold. In 1840 another Leicester entrepreneur, John Biggs, received a patent for making elastic-wristed gloves, and within four years he had 330 frames manufacturing them.

By 1861 there were twenty firms in the area and by 1877 there were forty-seven. The popularity of elastic-sided boots – easy to pull on and off, a bit like modern 'slip-on' shoes – increased demand, and for a time it was a profitable industry paying high wages, but by the 1880s elastic-sided boots were going out of fashion and the industry declined.

77. Elastic-sided boots of white satin. These used elastic web and were very popular in the middle years of the century. Unfortunately, elastic perishes, so the boots have lost the neat appearance they would have had when new.

Aniline Dyes

Up until the mid-nineteenth century, almost all dyes were natural, being made from vegetables, minerals and occasionally, animals. These dyes were often fugitive, and those made from certain substances that were rare or time-consuming to collect, for example insects and shellfish (for cochineal red and 'Tyrian' purple), were very expensive.

In 1856 William Henry Perkin, a young chemistry student, trying to create a chemical version of quinine – much needed by servants of the British Empire in the tropics – had the idea of using one of his failed experiments for another purpose. The result was something he called 'mauveine', which was based on aniline – a common extract of coal tar – and created a brilliant purple. Mauveine would lead the way to dyes in dozens of other shades, all made from aniline; 'Nicholson's blue' was particularly popular, as was 'Magenta', named after the Italian battle.

78. *Above and opposite*: Examples of fabrics dyed with aniline dyes, 1860s and '70s.

Crinolines

The word 'crinoline' derives from the French 'crin', which means 'horsehair', because some of the first petticoats designed to make the skirt stand out from the body were made of horsehair. The steel-hooped cage crinoline was patented in April 1856 by R. C. Milliet in Paris, and came to Britain a few months later. Factories across the western world were soon producing tens of thousands of crinoline cages a year in various sizes – the largest

Emily. *" Madame Bonton says 'the Circumference of the Crinoline should be Thirty-Six Feet!'"*
Caroline. *" Dear me!—I'm only Thirty-Two—I must Inflate a little!"*

79. *Punch* cartoon, 17 January 1857. Inflatable crinolines were a cartoonist's invention!

Leicestershire Journal, 3 March 1865.

could be 2 metres in diameter. They were a ridiculous fashion, but they were extremely popular in all strata of society, and they gave rise to a huge number of related inventions.

On 1 October 1859 the *Leicester Mercury* informed its readers that, 'There are few inventions which have given rise in so short a time to so many patents as the crinoline. It came into vogue only about four years ago, and already 100 patents have been taken out in France.' Folding crinolines were among the most popular of these many inventions, for obvious reasons.

Rubberised Fabrics

James Syme, a medical student, had found that coal tar naphtha was a good solvent for rubber. Charles Macintosh, an industrial chemist in Glasgow, used the naphtha-based rubber solution as a waterproofing layer between two fabrics. The best known use of this was for waterproof 'mackintoshes' – a term we still use today – but the fabric was also used for hats, aprons, underarm pads for dresses and a range of other items.

Chas. MACINTOSH & CO.

PATENTEES

OF

Indian Rubber
WATER-PROOF CLOTHS,

OF

DOUBLE TEXTURE.
AIR CUSHIONS, PILLOWS, &c.

46, CHEAPSIDE,
AND 58, CHARING CROSS, LONDON.

And at the Manufactory, Manchester.

CAUTION.

Chas. MACINTOSH & Co. having ascertained that spurious Articles have been sold as Improved Macintosh Garments, think it due to the Public and themselves to state, that none are genuine which have not the Autograph *C. Macintosh & Co.* engraved with the Royal Arms on the lining, as they send out none without this stamp.

(*See Vignette, and 58, in the Engraving.*)

PATENTEES OF INDIAN RUBBER WATER PROOF CLOTHS . OF DOUBLE TEXTURE . AIR CUSHIONS . PILLOWS &c. 58, CHARING CROSS & 46 , CHEAPSIDE, LONDON.

80. Advertisement for Charles Macintosh's shop and products.

81. *Punch* cartoon, 22 December 1883. Waterproof fabric was popularly believed to protect against germs.

Celluloid

The first synthetic plastic, celluloid was developed in the 1860s and 1870s from a homogeneous colloidal dispersion of nitrocellulose and camphor. It was tough and flexible, easy to mould, was resistant to water, could be made in a variety of colours and was cheap to produce. It was used for toiletry articles, novelties, toys, photographic film and many other mass-produced items, including dress accessories.

82. Silk blouse, *c.* 1900.

82a. Celluloid struts used to support the high neck of the silk blouse.

Tin-Weighted Silk

Silk was often treated to increase its weight and make it appear better quality – and thus more expensive – than it actually was. This type of processing started with vegetable-based solutions like tannins or sugar. Chemical solutions based on salts of lead or tin were then used, as well as phosphate of soda and silicates. Weighting made the silk drape well and caused it to rustle attractively as the wearer moved. By the 1880s and '90s this process was used excessively, with the result that many silk garments of that date are now brittle and disintegrating because, over time, the metallic salts have attacked the fabric.

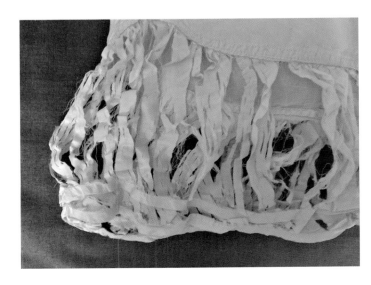

83. Detail of a petticoat flounce. The petticoat dates from the 1890s and is still in good condition but the flounce at the hem was obviously treated with an oxide of tin and is in ribbons.

Chapter 5

Trade

Queen Victoria ruled 'the empire on which the sun never set', and throughout the nineteenth century Britain traded, usually on very favourable terms, with most of the rest of the world. This, too, is reflected in what ladies wore.

Printed cottons, fine muslins and woven and embroidered shawls came from India and were hugely popular in the late eighteenth and early nineteenth century. They spawned copycat industries in the UK; fine white-work embroidery in Ayrshire and Ireland and shawl weaving in Paisley and Norwich, for example.

France was seen as the fashion centre of the world, and French silks, laces, fashion ideas and information had been imported into Britain for centuries. In the nineteenth century, high-class provincial dressmakers visited Paris at least once a year to bring news and samples of the latest modes back to their customers. In May 1853, for example, Priscilla Bark (see page 50) announced that she had, 'Just returned from PARIS with a choice selection of Novelties in MIILLINERY, MANTLES, DRESS MODELS, &c, &c, she will be fully prepared to show them on TUESDAY, the 10th of May, when she solicits a continuance of [her customers] kind patronage.'

84. Detail of a cotton fabric printed in India.

85. Detail of the corner of an embroidered Indian shawl.

86. Detail of a Chinese embroidered shawl, late nineteenth century.

There was a certain cachet attached to wearing items imported from France – shoes, fans, laces and so on – but English ladies also developed a taste for exotic items from further afield.

Anthony Trollope lampooned this in *The Struggles of Brown, Jones and Robinson, by One of the Firm*, a short story written in 1870. Brown, Jones and Robinson ran a department store.

Very many articles were asked for, looked at, and then not purchased ... The first article demanded over the counter was a real African monkey muff, very superior, with long fine hair. 'The ships which are bringing them have not yet arrived from the coast,' answered Jones ... 'They are expected in the docks tomorrow.'

Above: 87. Pair of glacé kid evening shoes, 1870s, by F. Pinet of Paris.

Left: 87a. Detail of the sole, which shows they were awarded a bronze medal at the Paris International exhibition of 1867.

Trollope was poking fun at the extravagance and dishonesty of contemporary advertising, ridiculing the credulity of shoppers – and elsewhere in the story, warning about banking and business practices. Unfortunately, 'real African monkey muffs' were not an invention; the colobus monkey, native to African forests, was hunted mercilessly for its distinctive black and white fur. On 24 November 1860, for example, John Brady on Gallowtree Gate advertised in the Leicester press that he had a large stock of both opossum and monkey muffs. Furs and skins of other sorts came from all over the world. Nineteenth-century ladies had few qualms about wearing fur; it was a status symbol and announced to the world that the wearer was a rich woman, or had at least had the good sense to marry a wealthy husband.

Similarly, they were quite happy to wear the feathers and the carcasses of brightly coloured birds, usually on their heads. As a result, some birds were hunted almost to extinction, like the American snowy egret, a little heron with pure white feathers. On 6 September 1856, for example, the *Leicester Mercury* fashion column informed its readers that, 'Small birds of Paradise will, it is expected, be much in favour this autumn. We have already seen them worn with good taste on rice straw or chip bonnets.' The hunters of Papua New Guinea, eastern Australia and Indonesia were set to profit.

Silk, both as fibre and fabric, or made into shawls, was imported in large quantities and the state of the Chinese silk harvest was a matter of some concern to traders in the UK. Ivory from African and Indian elephants was carved into jewellery, sticks and

88. Muff made from the fur of the Colobus monkey. This actually dates from the 1950s!

88a. Colobus monkey.

89. Muff of beaver fur, with its original box, from the late nineteenth century. The fur was probably imported from Canada.

90. Sable muff with tassels, nineteenth century. The sable is a member of the marten family and comes from Russia. The tassels are softer and are probably made from dyed rabbit fur.

91. Large bonnets like this were very fashionable in the late 1820s and early 1830s. This one is trimmed with ostrich feathers that were imported from Africa and dyed.

guards for fans and handles for parasols; 'tortoiseshell' from the hawksbill sea turtle (found in the Atlantic and the Pacific) made combs and other ornaments; bamboo from the Far East was used for canes and umbrellas and sunshades. When the Japanese began to trade with the west again in the 1880s, for a time Japanese paper fans and parasols were all the rage. Novelty and rarity were key selling points, and the ladies of Leicestershire were as anxious to be at the forefront of this fashion as anyone else. For example, on 27 December 1873, R. Curtis, who had a shop in Leicester Market Place, advertised card cases and fashion accessories 'in silver, pearl, ivory, tortoiseshell, sealskin and all kinds of leather' as acceptable, if rather belated, Christmas presents.

Again, the purpose of this chapter is to show examples rather than to give a complete overview of all the various items that might have been imported.

92. Parasol with an ivory handle engraved with a dragon, 1870s.

92a. Detail of the handle.

93. 'Brisé' fan of carved ivory, 1820s. 'Brisé' is the term for a fan without a leaf.

94. Tortoiseshell comb.

95. Chinese fan with ivory sticks and guards, mid-nineteenth century.

96. Fan with mother-of-pearl sticks and guards, late nineteenth century.

97. Japanese paper fan, late nineteenth century.

Chapter 6

The Changing Role of Women

For centuries, the restricted nature of women's social position was reflected and reinforced by the clothes they wore. Of course, working women had always adapted their dress a little – wearing their skirts a little shorter than their betters and covering them with voluminous aprons – but English working-class women were noted for their attempts to follow fashion. Indeed, those women whose occupations precluded them from dressing 'respectably' were despised. Ludicrous as it seems today, one of the objections to women hauling trucks in the mines was not the backbreaking labour, but the fact that they stripped to the waist to work and were seen in this state by their male colleagues.

There had always been a handful of women who adopted male dress, out of sheer eccentricity, in a genuine attempt to pass as male or as temporary protection when travelling alone, but for most of their contemporaries such behaviour was shocking in the extreme. However uncomfortable or ridiculous fashion might be, the vast majority of women dressed as convention dictated they should – even if they grumbled about it in private. But by the middle of the nineteenth century a small cohort of brave souls were seeking to change hearts and minds. One of the most famous of their number was Mrs Amelia Bloomer, an American who advocated a short version of the prevailing full-skirted dress to be worn over baggy, Turkish-style trousers. The ladies of Leicestershire were not left in ignorance of her ideas; lectures were given and articles were published, but it would seem that the ladies of the town and county were too conservative, or too fearful of ridicule, to adopt such radical proposals.

It would be another thirty years before another concerted attempt was made to persuade women to wear more practical outfits, this time by Viscountess Harberton and Mrs King, founders of the 'Rational Dress Society' (1881), but their success was also extremely limited. They advocated boneless corsets – available through the society – and fewer undergarments. They thought 7 lbs of underwear was more than sufficient; the average woman in the 1880s wore 14 lbs![18]

Sport was the way forward. To a limited extent, physicians supported the idea that their female patients should become more active: women rode horses, sea bathing was fashionable, a decorous game of tennis was in order, schools began to teach gymnastics and, in the 1880s and '90s, the arrival of the 'safety bicycle' turned cycling from a sport pursued by reckless young men into a useful means of transport for both sexes.

98. *Punch* cartoon, 3 October 1857. Male assistants working in a haberdashery department were thought to be effeminate and the cartoon implies they should be recruited into the army, while 'masculine' women, one of whom wears the outfit advocated by Amelia Bloomer, could take their places.

99. *Punch* cartoon, 14 November 1857. Ladies had ridden and hunted for centuries, but riding habits that consisted of a skirt over trousers were relatively new. Women and trousers were an irresistible combination for nineteenth-century cartoonists.

ANOTHER 'BLOOMER' IN LEICESTER – Mrs Horner, from Manchester, read a lecture on Reform in Female Dress at the New Hall, on Wednesday evening. Mrs H. was attired in a short dress and striped trousers, but looked much less attractive than Mrs Dexter, who lectured in the same place last week. The curiosity of the Leicester public appears to have been allayed by the first lecture, for the audience on Wednesday evening was very small. Mrs H. condemned long dresses, tight stays, and tight shoes. On Thursday morning Mrs H. promenaded some of the principal streets in the town in the new costume, and attracted a large concourse of youths, who gave her three cheers as she went into Cook's Boarding House. The vicinity of this house was crowded with spectators for two or three hours afterwards, and it was found necessary to send two policemen to keep the footpath clear. Mrs H. would lecture at Loughborough last night.

Leicester Journal, 14 November 1851.

However, appropriate clothing was always a problem. In the 1860s Mrs Sarah Evans' riding habit consisted of:

[A] fine dark blue cloth skirt about a foot below her feet, pleated all round into waist, no gore at all, a well cut bodice, little cloth buttons down front, a long basque, a soft white muslin chemisette, large felt hat trimmed with blue velvet leaves edged with little soft feathers, broad black ribbon strings tied under chin. She looked charming – the habit, tailor made, all by hand, lined silk.

However, it was deeply impractical, and one day she and her friend 'abstracted two pairs of trousers from Uncle's wardrobe, and donned them [under their habits, of course] to their own intense amusement'.[19]

In 1863 Louie Rayner's father agreed to take her and her sister to Norway on two conditions – one, that they learned to swim, and two, that they wore dresses suitable for walking and climbing:

We said that we could swim, but the second condition needed much more consideration. … No modest girl admitted to having two legs, and a pair of unabashed knickerbockers was not to be thought of. However, the costume that eventually emerged included blue serge knickers, duly abashed by a double skirt of the same material. When I say a double skirt, I mean the upper skirt was of conventional length and in no way remarkable; when adapted for serious walking it was coyly looped up over the underskirt, which was just above boot-tops.[20]

Louie's letter to Isabel actually gives the date of this excursion as 1883, but by then Louie was thirty-eight, twelve years married and the mother of young children, so it seems to be a misprint.

100. A bathing costume of navy serge trimmed with white braid, late nineteenth century.

101. A gymnastics class at the North London Collegiate School for Girls. The school was founded by Miss Mary Buss in 1850 and was a 'progressive' school for girls. *The Girl's Own Paper*, May 1882.

102. Ladies skating. This illustrated a feature on new outdoor clothes in *The Girl's Own Paper* for December 1881.

AMENITIES OF THE TENNIS-LAWN.

She. "YOURS OR MINE, SIR CHARLES!"   *He.* "YOURS—AW'FLY YOURS!"

Above left: 103. *Punch* cartoon, 13 October 1883. Playing mixed doubles was often an excuse for young people to spend time together unchaperoned.

Above right: 104. Sports corset, *c.* 1900, by Symingtons of Market Harborough. It is cut 'low under the bust, to allow for full circular arm movement', and 'high over the hip, for riding side-saddle and to allow the wearer to run and pedal a cycle'.

THE POINT OF VIEW.

Miranda. "HOW DELICIOUS THESE MOUNTAIN EXCURSIONS ARE! ONE FEELS SO COOL, SO FREE, SO UNTRAMMELLED!"   *Ferdinand.* "———!"

105. *Punch*, Christmas 1895.

Gradually, special garments became available commercially for a range of sports. Today we would balk at the idea of learning to swim in a heavy serge garment that enveloped the wearer from neck to mid-calf, but in the 1870s young women accepted it as the norm. Girls at school wore short loose dresses for 'drill' or sedate gymnastics. Tennis dresses were usually a version of fashionable dress, complete with frills and bustles. Women skied and skated wearing long skirts, and some even climbed mountains in them.

Cycling was a different matter and women cycling in long skirts were putting themselves at risk. Something more masculine that would not get entangled in the wheels or chain was needed and the Rational Dress Society advocated a divided skirt worn under a long jacket. Women wearing such outfits were ridiculed – Lady Harberton herself was refused entry to the dining room of the Hautboy Hotel in Ockham, Surrey, when she tried to go in for lunch wearing her cycling clothes in April 1899. She took the (female) hotel keeper to court – the case aroused considerable interest but was eventually dismissed. However, most women were less confident, and less wealthy, and many continued to wear skirts for cycling, sometimes with breeches underneath.

As more and more women took part in sport, Symingtons, and other firms, developed 'sports corsets', which were cut low under the arm and high over the hip to allow freer movement of the limbs. All these developments were widely ridiculed, particularly in *Punch,* hence the number of cartoons included in the illustrations to this section. Women's emancipation, however limited, was seen as a threat to the social order and was mercilessly mocked.

From the 1870s there was another sort of movement for less constricting dresses. This was the vogue in some circles for 'aesthetic dress' following the principles laid down by the Pre-Raphaelites for flowing dresses and un-corseted figures. Few outside their immediate circle followed these principles to the letter; there are a number of surviving dresses that have 'artistic' decoration but are in fact just as restrictive as fashionable outfits. Seen below is one such – the dress was worn by Mary Annie Sloane, who was a friend of William Morris's daughter, May, and it is believed that May Morris either did or designed the embroidery. The dress seems to be based on a romanticised version of medieval costume, but underneath the bodice is as fiercely boned as any other dress of the 1890s. Mary Annie was a talented artist, one of the five children of a surgeon at

106. *Punch*, 21 August 1875. The new-fangled bicycles provided a fresh form of amusement, though this image is obviously a cartoonist's invention.

Daughter (enthusiastically). "OH, MAMMA! I *MUST* LEARN BICYCLING! SO DELIGHTFUL TO GO AT SUCH A PACE!"
Mamma (severely). "NO THANK YOU, MY DEAR; YOU ARE *QUITE* 'FAST' ENOUGH ALREADY!"

Above: 107. *Punch*, 18 May 1895. Cycling gave women unprecedented freedom, which their elders found deeply troubling.

Below left: 108. *Punch*, 12 January 1895. Modern young women were anxious for clothes that gave them greater freedom, whatever the pretext!

Below right: 109. Dress in 'medieval' style, 1890s. It is made of white silk trimmed with braid and hand-embroidered, and with highly impractical 'hanging sleeves'. It was owned by Mary Annie Sloane, a friend of May Morris, who either designed or did the embroidery.

Gertrude. "MY DEAR JESSIE, WHAT ON EARTH IS THAT BICYCLE SUIT FOR!"
Jessie. "WHY, TO WEAR, OF COURSE." *Gertrude.* "BUT YOU HAVEN'T GOT A BICYCLE!"
Jessie. "NO; BUT I'VE GOT A SEWING MACHINE!"

Above & below: 109a and b. Details of the embroidery.

110. Mary Annie Sloane.

Leicester Infirmary. She never married, and spent many years working in London, but in old age she moved back to Leicestershire and lived at Enderby.

By the 1880s and '90s, taking a job outside the home was becoming increasingly acceptable, and women developed what was almost a uniform – a long dark skirt and a light coloured blouse, which could be frilly and lace trimmed or plain and severe, worn with boots in which the wearer could actually walk. There would be corsets and layers of underwear underneath, but at last women had clothes that were relatively practical. Such outfits were worn by working women, factory girls, countrywomen and respectable ladies alike.

Increasingly, women chafed against their subservient position, and an increasing number of them sought the right to vote like their husbands and sons. The National Union of Women's Suffrage Societies was founded in 1872. In Leicester, the leader of the Suffragette movement was Alice Hawkins. Born in 1863 in Stafford, she moved to Leicester with her family as a teenager and left school at thirteen to spend her working life as a shoe machinist. She soon realised that pay and working conditions for women in the industry were even worse than those for men, which led her to join the boot and shoe trade union. In her early twenties she was lucky enough to get a job in the Equity Shoe factory, which had been set up as a worker's co-operative and actively encouraged workers to participate in political organisations.

However, Alice gradually became disillusioned with the union, and in February 1907 she attended her first meeting of the Women's Social and Political Union (WSPU) in Hyde Park, followed by a march the same day to the House of Commons to demand the vote for women. That afternoon Alice was arrested and imprisoned along with several others. In the following seven years she would be arrested and jailed a total of five times, spending time in both Leicester and Holloway jails. Alice's first term of imprisonment

Right: 111. Blouse and skirt, 1890s.

Below: 112. Embroidered blouse of fine muslin, early twentieth century.

113. Cotton blouse, *c.* 1900. This is a working woman's version of the prevailing fashion.

114. Miss Lumbers, wearing the ubiquitous blouse and skirt combination, early twentieth century. Her father, John Lumbers, was a watchmaker and jeweller and the family lived at 28 Granby Street, Leicester.

115. Haymakers at Bitteswell, *c.* 1900. The women of the family are watching the haymakers leave for the fields and are dressed in their everyday blouses and skirts.

had a profound effect upon her and the next month she invited Sylvia Pankhurst to speak in Leicester. Shortly after that, the Leicester section of the WSPU was formed.[21]

One early suffragette was a young school teacher called Susanne Potter. Years later she would admit that what really attracted her to the movement was the license to be 'really naughty' and she took great delight in pouring glue into letter boxes and breaking windows! She saved up to buy an elaborate cream coat dress, trimmed with braid, which she wore with a sash in the suffragette colours of purple, green and white, and a large hat. She was wearing it on the day she was imprisoned in Holloway following a demonstration. It remained a treasured possession, and finally, as an old lady, she proudly donated it to the museum collection.

While women's clothing was gradually becoming more practical there were still some setbacks for the fashion-conscious. Enormous hats which had to be skewered to the hair with hatpins remained fashionable, and for a short time in the 1910s 'hobble skirts' came into vogue. They were fashionably short in that they showed the wearer's ankles, and looked loose, but in fact the skirts had inner ties that narrowed them so much at knee level that walking became difficult.

By 1914 Britain was at war, and it was a war that impacted heavily on the civilian population. With the unprecedented slaughter at the Front and the endless calls for new cannon fodder, attitudes to women, work and what they wore at last began to change. In 1918, immediately after the war, Alice, Susanne and their companions had a partial success: the coalition government gave the vote to women over thirty, but it would be another decade before women would be allowed to vote on the same basis as men, at age twenty-one.

116. Suffragette dress, *c.* 1910–12, worn by Susanne Potter. It is made of fine cream wool and has elaborately braided trimming.

117. Leicester suffragettes in Belvoir Street.

118. *Punch* cartoon, 20 April 1910, making fun of the difficulties of walking in a hobble skirt.

However, the war, dreadful as it was, had given women unprecedented opportunities. For a few years, it was not only acceptable for gently born girls to work outside the home, it was seen as their patriotic duty. Things changed when the men who survived came home, but they would never be quite the same again, and whatever vagaries might be deemed fashionable in the twentieth century, never again would all women feel obliged to slavishly follow trends that put their lives, health and ability to move freely at risk.

Epilogue

Leicester may no longer be one of the wealthiest cities in Europe; indeed, recent studies have shown that some areas of the city are in fact among the most deprived in the UK. However, the inhabitants are still fashion-conscious, and the city's De Montfort University runs highly acclaimed design courses for fashion, shoes, textiles and 'contour fashion' (swimwear and corsetry), paying homage to the city's industrial past. Leicester's claim to fame in the early twenty-first century is that it was the first European city in which inhabitants of non-European origin outnumbered those from Europe and the UK. This means that the heart of the city is today a colourful place, in which saris, shalwar kameez, niqabs and bright African robes rub shoulders with jeans and t-shirts, outfits from Primark and smart business suits.

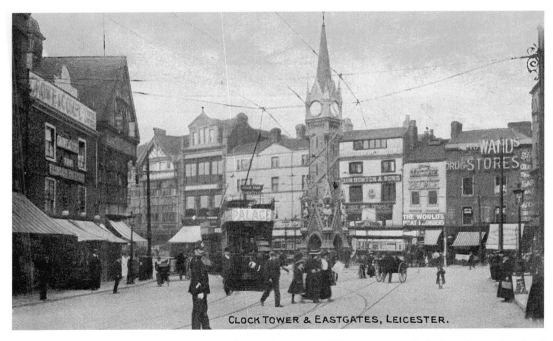

CLOCK TOWER & EASTGATES, LEICESTER.

119. Postcard of Leicester showing the clock tower and Eastgate shortly before the outbreak of the First World War. The shoppers are all quite fashionably dressed.

Sadly, none of the extensive costume collections belonging to Leicester and Leicestershire is on display at the time of writing. Wygston's House in Leicester, which used to house the costume collection, and where many of the photographs in this book were taken, has been sold and is now a restaurant. Much of the collection then moved to purpose-built display and storage accommodation at Snibston Discovery Park near Coalville, but the building that housed it has now been demolished to make way for a housing development. It is now at the Collections Resource Centre in Barrow-on-Soar, where items can be viewed on request, while the rest remains with the Leicester Arts and Museum Service. It is to be hoped that this book will serve as a reminder of the richness of both these collections.

References

1   Haynes, Barry, *Working-Class Life in Victorian Leicester: The Joseph Dare Reports* (1991).
2   Leicestershire Record Office, DG9/2302.
3   *Dressmakers' Chart and Cutting Guide*, 1888–9.
4   Evans, Isabel C., *Reports of Nineteenth Century Leicester* (1935).
5   Leicestershire Record Office, diaries and memoir, 7D54.
6   Foss and Parry (eds), *A Truly Honest Man* (1998).
7   *Leicester Journal*, 3 October 1862.
8   *Leicester Mercury*, 17 July 1858.
9   *Leicester Mercury*, May 1858.
10   *Leicester Mercury*, August 1857.
11   *Leicester Mercury*, January 1858.
12   Kirby, Mary, *Leaflets from my Life* (1888).
13   Evans, Isabel C., *Reports of Nineteenth Century Leicester* (1935).
14   Blow, M. M., *Diary of Ada Jackson* (1993).
15   Moore, Andrew, *Ellis of Leicester: A Quaker Family's Vocation* (2003).
16   Evans, Isabel C., *Reports of Nineteenth Century Leicester* (1935).
17   Leicestershire Record Office, D46/D262.
18   Pomeroy, Florence, *Reasons for Reform in Dress* (1884).
19   Evans, Isabel C., *Reports of Nineteenth Century Leicester* (1935).
20   Evans, Isabel C., *Reports of Nineteenth Century Leicester* (1935).
21   Whitmore, Richard, *Alice Hawkins and the Suffragette Movement in Edwardian Leicester* (2012).